HUNTING: PURSUING WILD GAME!™

HUNTING DOGS

DIFFERENT BREEDS AND SPECIAL PURPOSES

SUSAN MEYER

rosen publishing's
rosen
central®

New York

Published in 2013 by The Rosen Publishing Group, Inc.
29 East 21st Street, New York, NY 10010

First Edition

Library of Congress Cataloging-in-Publication Data

Meyer, Susan, 1986–
Hunting dogs: different breeds and special purposes/Susan Meyer.
    p. cm.—(Hunting—pursuing wild game!)
Includes bibliographical references and index.
ISBN 978-1-4488-8276-2 (library binding: alk. paper)—
ISBN 978-1-4488-8281-6 (pbk.: alk. paper)—
ISBN 978-1-4488-8282-3 (6-pack: alk. paper)
1. Hunting dogs—Juvenile literature. I. Title.
SF428.5.M49 2013
636.75—dc23

2012018939

Manufactured in the United States of America

CPSIA Compliance Information: Batch #W13YA: For further information, contact Rosen Publishing, New York, New York, at 1-800-237-9932.

On the cover: A well-trained and well-chosen hunting dog is both a superb worker and a perfect companion.

CONTENTS

*H*umankind has been hunting for all of its history. Early humans had to hunt to obtain the food necessary for survival. These prehistoric humans didn't have the equipment that modern hunters rely on today. However, while guns and ammunition are a fairly recent addition to hunting, humans have been getting some help from a certain furry friend for almost twenty thousand years. Early hunters, who did not have sophisticated weapons for harvesting game, used dogs to locate prey and allow them to get close enough to use nets or bows and arrows. These original hunting companions were mostly domesticated wolves. However, in all that time, the human species has evolved a lot, and so have the dogs with which they hunt.

As humans discovered other sources of food, hunting became less of a means of survival and more of a sport. This development also changed the type of dogs that were needed for the hunt. Humans began breeding dogs with specific traits. Some dogs were bred to have a perfect sense of smell to track game. Others were bred to be incredibly fast to pursue game over great distances. Still others were bred to be strong swimmers who could retrieve game that had fallen into water.

People have aided the evolution of hunting dogs by breeding them for desired traits. Greyhounds, like the one seen here, are a breed known for their incredible speed.

Today, there are hundreds of different breeds of hunting dogs. Some of them are still used primarily for hunting. Others are mostly retired from hunting but are still useful as service dogs and household pets.

Owning a hunting dog can be the basis for an amazing partnership. A well-trained dog is a huge asset to any hunter. However, owning, training, and maintaining a hunting dog are also big responsibilities. Dogs have been helping people hunt for much of human history, so it's only fitting that they get their due.

CHAPTER 1

HISTORY AND EVOLUTION OF HUNTING DOGS

No history of the sport of hunting would be complete without an examination of the contributions dogs have offered to human hunters for centuries. There is evidence of wolves being domesticated for human use in hunting more than twenty thousand years ago. These dogs were extremely helpful in the survival of early man. At that time, the hunt was less about the thrill of the sport and far more about survival. Humans depended on the animals they harvested for their food, for their clothing, and sometimes for the shelters they lived in.

This relief, currently in the British Museum, dates from 650 BCE and shows ancient Assyrian hunters with their dogs leaving for a hunt.

Wolves Join the Human Pack

Dogs evolved after modern humans were already in existence, so there was a period of human history in which dogs did not exist. There were plenty of wolves, jackals, and coyotes, but no dogs as we know them today. While wolves are closely related to dogs and resemble them somewhat, there are many key differences between the two species. Wolves live in the wild and hunt, usually in groups, to provide themselves with

Wolves are the ancestors of early dogs, but today the animals are two distinct species. Wolves, like the one seen here enjoying its kill, hunt in packs for food.

food. On the other hand, dogs tend to live around humans and look to them to provide food. Dogs, as we know them today, seem naturally inclined to be social toward humans.

This domestication did not happen overnight. In fact, it may have taken hundreds of years for wild animals to form a completely new species—genetically separate from wolves—that today we call dogs. These early dogs helped human hunters in a variety of ways. Sometimes humans would dig pit traps into which dogs would chase the game. Dogs could also flush out game so that hunters could shoot it with arrows or spears.

Dogs in the Ancient World

We know that hunting dogs were important to early humans, but we can also see evidence of this in the artifacts of the ancient civilizations. The ancient Sumerian *Epic of Gilgamesh*, one of the oldest stories we have today, dating from 2000 BCE, mentions a goddess owning seven prized hunting dogs. In ancient Egypt, dogs were considered such an important part of the household that those families who could afford it would often mummify a dog on its death. These mummified dogs and even some of their collars have been found preserved in Egyptian tombs.

In Greek myth, you may have heard of the great hunter Orion, who provides the name for one of the most recognizable constellations visible from all over the world. However, you might not be as familiar with two nearby constellations: Canis Major and Canis Minor. These are the names of Orion's two hunting dogs. So on a clear night, you need look no farther than the sky to see two of the earliest celebrity hunting dogs.

Over ten thousand years ago, humans began to grow crops and domesticate livestock—like sheep and goats—to eat. This made hunting less of a necessity for survival. Domesticated dogs were then used less often for hunting and more frequently for herding livestock to keep it from running off or to protect it from wolves and wild dogs.

As agriculture really took off, hunting became more of a sport than a requirement for survival, and the role of dogs in hunting evolved further. Hunting dogs were developed to track and point out game to their owners. Skeletal remains indicate that five very different types of dog existed around the year 4,500 BCE. These included mastiffs, wolf-type dogs, greyhounds, pointing dogs, and shepherding dogs. In addition to these fossil records, there are cave paintings that show dogs working alongside human hunters.

The Earliest Breeders

It wasn't too long after domesticating dogs that humans began to intentionally create new breeds. Humans shaped the evolution of dogs by

The ancient Romans were some of the earliest dog breeders. They bred dogs to make them better hunting companions. This mosaic found near modern Sicily dates from between 285 and 305 CE.

selecting those dogs that had traits that they wanted over others that didn't. They would mate two dogs that both showed the traits they wanted—be it good eyesight or hardiness—in the hopes that the resulting puppies would also have these traits. The early Greeks and Romans devoted a great deal of time to training dogs for hunting as well as breeding them to bring out certain characteristics. In directing the evolution of the species, humans developed several distinct canine bloodlines that can be divided into the earliest breeds of hounds, some of which are still in existence today.

Hounds were the first kings of the hunt with their keen senses and powerful athleticism. No less important in the hunting world, although much closer to the ground, are the smaller hunting dogs—the terriers and dachshunds—who are small but feisty. These dogs burrow right into an animal's den to confront the prey on its own turf. When guns were invented, a new group of dogs came onto the scene, collectively known as gun dogs. These dogs were bred to satisfy a whole new host of needs that arose from being able to dispatch prey from greater distances.

Although breeding has its advantages because it has created dogs that are uniquely suited for very specific hunting needs, it also has its drawbacks. Purebred dogs, in addition to the positive characteristics that define their breed, might also have certain inherited characteristics that can develop into a disability or disease. These conditions might include excessive wear on the hip bones, back issues, or eye troubles that could keep the dog from being able to hunt or even able to get around very well later in life. Heart conditions might also be inherited, which can shorten the life of the dog. There have been extensive studies of these conditions, and much of this data has been recorded as part of the information available on a breed. This is one of the many reasons why, when you decide you want to get a dog, it is so important to research your chosen breed first. Checking the dog's pedigree will help determine any inherited issues the dog may have as well. Every dog registered with the American Kennel Club will have this, tracked back many generations on the dam (mother's) and sire's (father's) side.

Over time, the specific characteristics and purposes for which certain hunting dogs were bred have been ingrained into the particular breed, and these traits and behaviors have actually become part of their nature. This explains why Labradors, who were bred to retrieve game like ducks and to fetch fishing nets, love water and playing retrieving games such as fetch. It also explains why Jack Russells, who are terriers bred to chase game from their dens, cannot resist a good hole or chasing any squirrel in sight. And it explains why beagles, who are actually a kind of hound, will run off after certain types of prey and have such loud, alarm-raising barks.

CHAPTER 2

HOUNDS OF THE HUNT

Hounds are the original hunting dog. Some hounds have an acute sense of smell that they use for following the trail of quarry. Others have extreme speed and stamina to help them run down game. There is a great deal of diversity within the group known as hounds. They are usually used in hunting to pursue quarry over long distances. Sometimes they will dispatch the prey themselves, and sometimes they will hold it down until their human hunting companion arrives.

The two main groups, sighthounds and scenthounds, have been around for thousands of years. A third group of hounds, known as treeing hounds, have been bred relatively recently in North America for hunting animals that try to escape by running up trees.

Keeping Prey in Sight

Sighthounds are appropriately named as they are slender, elongated, speedy athletes who track prey by sight rather than scent. Collectively, this group of canines has gone by many names: sighthounds, gaze-hounds, and windhounds. These swift-footed dogs hunt by chasing down, catching, and either killing their prey or securing it until the human hunter arrives. This type of hunting—pursuing game with dogs as the primary weapon—is called coursing. Originally, coursing was a type of hunting practiced by nobility.

Sighthounds must have a keen sense of vision to detect motion. Sighthounds are serious athletes that must be able to catch very speedy prey like rabbits and deer. They have a deep chest to support a large heart, long legs, and a flexible back so that they can run fast and have a long stride. They also usually have very efficient lungs to make it easier for them to sprint. There are a number of different breeds of sight-hounds, many of which you would probably recognize. These include the greyhound, the Irish wolfhound, and the saluki.

The greyhound is a super speedy dog that can run up to 39 miles (63 kilometers) per hour. Originally, greyhounds were primarily bred in the British Isles and in Europe for the coursing of deer. Later, they were used for coursing rabbits. Greyhounds have the longest history of any breed of hunting dog, as they are depicted in ancient art from six thousand years ago. In early centuries, greyhounds were owned exclusively by nobles. Today, greyhounds participate both in coursing and racing competitions to show off their great speed. Despite their fast-paced lives, greyhounds actually have very relaxed personalities. They also make very gentle and obedient pets.

While the greyhound is the fastest dog, the Irish wolfhound has the distinction of being the tallest. It is believed that these dogs

This greyhound is participating in an annual coursing event called the Waterloo Cup. In this competition, greyhounds compete against each other to chase hares.

were brought to Europe more than three thousand years ago by the ancient Phoenicians. They were originally bred to protect livestock from wolves, which is where they get their name. However, they were also used to hunt elk and wolves. These dogs usually hunted alone or in pairs instead of in packs, which is why their great size is so important. When elk and wolves became extinct in Ireland, the Irish

Hounds on the Fox Hunt

Fox hunting is a sport that involves the tracking, chasing, and sometimes killing of a fox. This feat is performed by a pack of trained foxhounds or other scenthounds and a group of unarmed followers who follow the hounds on horseback or sometimes on foot. Fox hunting became very popular in England toward the end of the seventeenth century, when deer numbers were in decline. This was around the time that the American colonies were founded, so it was only a matter of time before the practice of hunting hounds crossed the Atlantic. The first pack of hunting dogs was brought to Maryland in 1650 by a man named Robert Brooke. George Washington and Thomas Jefferson were both fans of fox hunting. Today, the foxhound is even the state dog of Virginia.

Many people have spoken out against fox hunting, calling it a cruel sport. New laws in the United States and England have made illegal most forms of fox hunting, whose intent is the killing of the fox. However, in both countries, people still enjoy fox hunting today. In some cases they will still chase a fox but stop after it goes into hiding, which is known as "going to ground." Another method that fox hunting clubs in Virginia use is called drag hunting. In a drag hunt, there is no live quarry, but the pack follows a scent that was previously laid down by people who drag a scented bag across the hunt area.

wolfhound began to die out, too, but breeders have made efforts to revive the breed.

The saluki is another sighthound with quite a long history. These long-legged and long-eared hounds are thought to have been around since 7,000 BCE. These dogs are both intelligent and independent, and they need to draw upon both qualities to master the style in which they usually hunt. Salukis are used in small packs to hunt game. They have to act with cunning and skill to capture the prey. The dog's job is to pursue the prey, racing at incredible speeds to capture it and hold it down until the hunter arrives. This is because where salukis were raised, in the deserts of the Middle East, the hunter, not the dog, must be the one who harvests the game if it is to be eaten. This practice derives from religious dietary laws.

Follow Your Nose

If sighthounds are the sprinters of the hound world, scenthounds are the marathon runners. These stocky, athletic dogs often have drooping ears and smooth coats. Many breeds have a tricolor pattern in their coats of white with black and brown patches. But the most important feature of the scenthound, as you might imagine, is its highly sensitive nose. If you see a scenthound on the hunt, you will notice it is frequently rushing this way and that with its nose to the ground, hoping to pick up the faintest of scents.

Scenthounds fall into three main categories, based on their appearance: large, heavy-bodied hounds; athletic, medium-built hounds; and small, short-legged hounds. There are two types of hunting that scenthounds participate in: grande vénerie and petite vénerie. Grande vénerie means the hunting of large game like deer with a pack of hounds following the scent and pursuing their quarry to the end. Petite vénerie means hunting small game like rabbits, foxes, and birds, and using the scent to drive the quarry to the waiting huntsmen.

A familiar example of a large, heavy-bodied hound is the bloodhound. These, and other scenthounds in this category, are generally used to hunt in small numbers and are kept on a leash by the huntsman who pursues quarry on foot. For this reason, they are often known as leash-hounds. Bloodhounds have been around since the eleventh century, when they were brought to England by William the Conqueror. They were originally used for hunting deer because of their amazing sense of smell. They could follow the smell of a wounded deer over incredibly long distances. Over the centuries, the deer began to disappear, and foxes became the primary hunting target. With that change, bloodhounds weren't fast enough to keep up and were replaced by foxhounds as the primary scenthound. However, bloodhounds are still used today to track down missing persons and criminals. A good bloodhound can track a human scent that is more than twenty-four hours old over a distance of 3 miles (4.8 km).

A common example of an athletic, medium-bodied scenthound is the foxhound. As its name would suggest, these hounds were bred expressly to hunt foxes—originally in England, and later in the United States. The foxhound is built for stamina, and it can travel quickly over great distances. When out hunting, these dogs pursue their prey while being followed by human hunters, usually on horseback. Dogs like the foxhound are thus often called horse hounds. These dogs have strong natural instincts to hunt and are both energetic and active. They are still used all over the world to hunt today and are hardly ever seen as household pets.

The third type of scenthound is the short-legged variety. These include the beagle and the basset hound. These dogs hunt in groups off the leash and are followed by hunters on foot, so they are often called foot hounds. There are several advantages to using short-legged scenthounds and pursuing by foot, which have made these types of dogs popular through the centuries. For one, with no horses involved, the hunts are comparatively cheaper. Also, thanks to their short legs and low-slung bodies, these dogs can explore the ground cover and go places that taller dogs and hunters on horseback can't. Their short legs make them slower than other breeds of scenthounds. However, in some ways this, too, can be an advantage as game is driven forward at a slower pace and is not panicked out of the hunters' range.

When hunting with short-legged scenthounds, the dogs will either trail the quarry and drive it toward the hunters' guns or will pursue the quarry and kill it themselves. Beagles were

originally bred to hunt rabbits and hares and became popular as foot

A man on horseback leads a team of trained foxhounds on a traditional fox hunt in Gloucestershire in England. This man is appropriately called the master of the foxhounds.

hounds for those who couldn't afford hunting on horseback. They first came to the United States in 1876 and have since become a popular breed both for sporting and as household pets. The droopy-eared basset hound is another favorite short-legged scent hound. They are solemn, friendly dogs who become stubbornly single-minded when in pursuit of quarry on the hunt. They are also known for their deep and powerful bark.

Barking Up the Right Tree

The final types of hounds are known as treeing hounds. These dogs are primarily bred to hunt in the United States and Canada. In Europe, the quarry that are hunted are usually animals that go underground to escape dogs, such are rabbits, badgers, and foxes. However, hunters in North America soon discovered the presence of prey like raccoons

Bluetick hounds tree a raccoon while training for a treeing competition. These dogs specialize in chasing small animals up trees and keeping them there.

and opossums that escape by running up trees. Treeing hounds, sometimes called coonhounds, are trained to remain at the foot of a tree that their prey has run up. They will continue to wait, and sometimes bark, at the tree until the hunter can arrive and finish the kill.

Treeing hounds were bred from scenthounds that were brought to the United States as pack hunters. Originally, these dogs enjoyed the chase, and when the animal ran up a tree, they would lose patience and look for other quarry. By breeding those individual dogs that showed a greater stubbornness and refusal to give up on prey that had been treed, American and Canadian hunters eventually arrived at a whole new class of hounds. Some common treeing hounds include the blue tick coonhound and the black-and-tan coonhound, which is the oldest of the coonhound breeds.

In recent years, treeing dog competitions have become increasingly popular. There are three types of these trials. The first is the night hunt, in which rival dogs are sent after raccoons, which are nocturnal animals. The second is the drag hunt in which the competitors pursue a decoy scent that is dragged over a path on dry land. The third type of competition is a water race in which the dogs must pursue a scent across a river or other source of water.

CHAPTER 3

SMALL DOGS WITH BIG ABILITIES

Not all hunting dogs have long legs and deep barks. Some are small in size but are nevertheless powerful hunting machines. The dogs in this group include terriers, dachshunds, and feists. Many of these dogs have been used for hunting small game and for pest control for at least a thousand years.

When it comes to terriers and dachshunds, there are three ways that these dogs may hunt. The first is to enter the burrows of their prey and attack it underground. The second is to enter the burrow and scare the prey so that it runs above ground, where the hunters wait. The third method is to wait outside the burrow and dispatch the prey when it comes above ground. Not all small hunting dogs are burrowers though. There are several breeds of small hunting dogs called feists that also hunt animals that escape up trees instead of underground.

Terriers and Terriermen

Terriers are little dogs with big personalities. They are distinctively energetic and fearless. Most terriers have wiry coats that require special grooming in order to maintain their characteristic appearance. Most terrier breeds were developed in England and Ireland, where they were used to control rats, rabbits, foxes, and sometimes badgers and otters. They would pursue their prey underground. As a group, they are sometimes called earth dogs. The name "terrier" actually comes from the Latin word *terra*, or "earth." Many terriers, whose ancestors were bred to hunt and kill vermin, are now exclusively household pets. Other terrier breeds are still used in hunting today, but even these breeds make excellent pets. Terriers that are kept as pets are engaging and affectionate companions but require owners with determination to match their dogs' lively personalities.

Today, terriers are used by hunters called terriermen. These hunters dig holes to help reach the dens of groundhogs, raccoons, foxes, or even rats. They use terriers to help scare an animal out of a den. They often put locating collars on the terriers so that they can tell where a dog is while it's underground. Terriermen don't always harvest the game they hunt. Sometimes, they hunt just for sport and release the animals they find. Other times, they will be asked by farmers to help in removing groundhogs or other animals they consider pests. The work of terrier hunting is somewhat controversial because some people think it is cruel to hunt animals in their dens.

Terriers are usually classified by the type of prey they were bred to specialize in. Some familiar terriers include the fox terrier and Jack

This terrier is a dog working with a terrierman on a hunt in England. This dog was employed to dig out a fox that had gone to ground, or gone into hiding.

Russell terrier, bred to hunt foxes; the Airedale terrier, bred to hunt otters; and the rat terrier, fittingly bred to hunt rats.

Sausage-Shaped Badger Hunters

Dachshunds are one of the more instantly recognizable breeds due to their short legs and characteristically long bodies. They can have short, long, or wiry hair. The use of the term "hot dog" for a sausage in a bun stems from a 1903 cartoon showing one of these dogs on a bread roll.

Dachshunds are an interesting breed because, while they were bred to go underground like terriers, they are often classified with hounds. They do share some characteristics with hounds, and they occasionally hunt rabbits and hares by scent, as would a beagle. But they are considered more closely related to terriers because their primary function is going to ground. Part of the reason they may have been classified as hounds is because of

Edwin Megargee

This illustration shows three types of dachshunds—short-haired, long-haired, and wire-haired—doing what they do best: burrowing into a badger hole.

their name. *Dachshund* is German for "badger dog," but because of the similarity between the German word for dog, *hund*, and the English word "hound," they were sometimes mistakenly labeled the "badger hound."

In Germany, the earliest specific record of dachshunds dates from 1735, although this type of dog—with a long body and intentionally

Feist or Fiction?

Because feists are bred strictly for hunting and not for show, they are often less familiar outside the hunting community. However, these small treeing dogs make a number of appearances in both history and literature. George Washington wrote about a yellow feist in a diary entry in 1770. Another important American president, Abraham Lincoln, wrote about these dogs many years later in a poem called "The Bear Hunt." In the poem, "feist" is spelled "fice," and the dog is described as short-legged but fierce on the hunt.

Lincoln's poem is not the only instance of these small hunters appearing in literature. The Nobel Prize–winning American author William Faulkner wrote about them in a story in his 1942 collection of short fiction, *Go Down, Moses*. He describes a brave feist (which he spells "fyce") killed by a bear while on a hunt. Another well-known American author, Marjorie Kinnan Rawlings, mentions the hunting feist in her Pulitzer Prize–winning novel *The Yearling*. So while these short-statured dogs aren't as well known and immediately recognizable as some of the hounds or terriers, they have had an important place both in the world of hunting and in the world of literature.

shortened legs—had already been in existence for several centuries. They were bred to create a fearless, elongated dog that could dig the earth covering a badger burrow and fight to the death with the vicious creatures hidden inside. They soon arrived in England from Germany, and Queen Victoria owned these hot dog–shaped pups as early as the 1840s. The breed became popular in the United States in the early 1900s.

In addition to following badgers into burrows, dachshunds are occasionally used to hunt rabbits and foxes as well. Small dachshunds (those with a chest circumference 14 inches [36 centimeters] or less) are very useful for locating and confronting animals in their dens. Dachshunds have good noses and can accurately locate an animal underground. If the animal digs away from the dachshund, the dachshund, with experience, will be able to relocate it. Most small dachshunds are not so aggressive that they get seriously bitten by the animal, but they are keen enough to stay with their quarry underground.

Today, in the United States, dachshunds are occasionally still used for this style of hunting, although the typical prey are now woodchucks and groundhogs rather than badgers. In the American West, they were also sometimes used to eliminate prairie dogs.

Small and Feisty

A word that is often used to describe the tenacious personality of terriers and other small dogs is "feisty." The origin of this word is actually derived from several breeds of small dogs collectively known as feists. Feists are small—often shorter than 18 inches (45 cm) and weighing less than 30 pounds (14 kilograms). They are short-coated dogs, usually with bobtails. Because feists are not usually shown in dog shows and thus are not required to meet certain rigid aesthetic

A game warden and squirrel hunter is seen here working with two treeing feists while hunting game. Feists are silent during the hunt but bark for all they're worth as soon as their prey is treed.

standards, there is a great variation in their appearance. There are many different breeds of feists, from the mountain feist to the tree-ing feist and the Cajun squirrel dog.

Unlike many of the other small dogs, feists work aboveground to chase small prey, especially squirrels. Most feists have an incredible natural instinct to chase squirrels, rabbits, and rodents. When on the hunt, feists are silent until they sight a squirrel or other prey. Then they will tree the squirrel by barking loudly and circling around the tree. Feists practice a very similar style of hunting to treehounds, except that they are smaller and chase smaller game than hounds. A feist will chase a squirrel until it leaves its sight. It may wade through streams or leap through undergrowth to get to its quarry. Although feists are experts of the chase, they seldom catch and dispatch the prey themselves, unlike hounds. Instead, they usually wait until their owner makes the kill.

CHAPTER 4

GUN DOGS

*A*s hunting evolved to allow for firearms, so, too, did hunting dogs. Guns allowed hunters to shoot game—especially birds in flight—that were farther away. In many ways, guns have made hunting much easier for the hunter. However, they have also presented the new challenge of quietly locating prey that can be shot from a distance, without alerting it to the danger and scaring it off. Other times, as with birds, prey must be startled by the dog and take wing, offering hunters a clear shot. Another challenge is locating prey that has been shot from a distance and wounded or killed, and that may no longer be visible to the hunter.

To solve these problems, new breeds of dogs were trained to silently locate prey, flush prey, and/or retrieve dead game. This group of dogs is collectively known as

One way that gun dogs are useful to hunters is that they can flush out game from the ground, such as this pheasant, so that the hunter can make the kill.

gun dogs. Gun dogs are most easily subdivided into three categories: setters and spaniels that flush out the game from the ground; pointers that identify game to the hunter; and retrievers that fetch the felled game. Many dogs can be trained and are capable of doing all three tasks, but they are usually categorized by the task they specialize in.

Flushing Dogs

The role of the flushing dog is to search in fields and undergrowth for game, usually birds, and then scare it into fleeing from cover. Once the game leaves the safety of cover, the hunter can shoot it. The dog will then often locate the fallen game and retrieve it for the hunter. Flushing dogs have been around since before sporting guns were used in hunting. In medieval England, when these dogs flushed out game, it would be killed by the hunter's falcons. The typical flushing dog is the spaniel. However, while all flushing dogs are spaniels, not all spaniels are flushing dogs. Certain breeds, like the King Charles spaniel, are strictly household pets. The most common flushing dogs are the cocker spaniel and the springer spaniel.

Today, the cocker spaniel is one of the most popular of all spaniel breeds. With their small size, they can more easily fit into dense thickets to flush out game. Their current name is derived from their original name, woodcock spaniel (woodcocks were once their main quarry). These dogs are gentle and playful and have very friendly and affectionate personalities. They are also highly intelligent and curious and frequently serve as household pets.

Second only to the cocker spaniel in numbers is the springer spaniel, which was named for its ability to make game spring up out of hiding. It is a very athletic dog that requires a lot of daily physical activity to be happy.

Achieving Retrievers

Retrievers need to be on top of their game to be useful to a hunter in the field. There are a number of skills that a hunter must train his or her dog to acquire and practice and a number of commands to obey. A retriever must learn to sit calmly and under control for long periods of time before it retrieves something. It must remain steady even when a bird flies up or when a gun is fired. It also must mark downed game, meaning it pays very close attention to where a bird has fallen so that it can swim out to exactly where it fell.

Once the retriever actually swims out and finds the bird, it must deliver it back to the hunter with a soft mouth so as not to damage the game. The retriever is trained to drop the quarry only when commanded to do so by the hunter. Another important command every retriever must learn is to shake off water only when told. If you've ever seen a dog get out of the water, you know the first thing it wants to do is shake off. But if a retriever with a bird in its mouth were to do that, it could damage the game. Much of what a hunter must do when training his or her gun dog is to help it become used to situations on the hunt, like gunfire and other obstacles and distractions it might experience in a real-world hunting situation. The process of training a good gun dog can take a long time, but the reward is an invaluable hunting companion.

Pointers and Setters

The ancestors of modern pointing dogs were first bred in Europe in the seventeenth century. Back then, the guns being used were very inefficient compared to the guns used in hunting today. These early guns took a long time for the hunter to reload. The hunter needed

The Brittany is a breed of pointer. Here, a Brittany is frozen in place pointing at prey to keep it from moving until the hunter can arrive.

a dog that had extreme patience while locating prey and could freeze like a statue and point at the quarry. After the dog located game, it would stand perfectly still in what is called a "hold." This would give the hunter time to reload and keep the quarry from being startled and running away. The pointer would hold a precise pose with one front leg raised as if about to take another step until the hunter commanded the dog to move.

Pointing was a skill that took a lot of training and could be mastered by only the most patient and self-disciplined members of the breed. As guns improved and no longer required such a long time to load and reload in the eighteenth century, the role of the pointer also changed. They were bred to be smaller and quicker dogs to respond to the new style of hunting. Today, there are two types of pointers. The first group is designed only to point to game. The second group is more all-purpose and can hunt, point, and retrieve game. These dogs are sometimes referred to as HPR breeds (for hunt-point-retrieve).

Pointers vary widely in appearance. Some have long hair and others short. One thing most pointers have in common is that they have some sort of spots in their markings. They are generally very obedient, intelligent, and even-tempered dogs. Some familiar pointing dogs include the English pointer, which is sometimes simply referred to as a pointer and specializes in game birds, and the Weimaraner, a large

Retrievers are excellent swimmers and have a soft mouth, two qualities that help them fetch downed waterfowl and return them safely to the hunter.

gray dog that is capable of dealing with both large and small prey.

Similar to pointers in function are setters. These dogs search for prey, but when the quarry is detected, they don't run out to flush it. Instead, they freeze and "set" their body in the direction of the hiding prey. Setters are traditionally thought to be descended from spaniel breeds and are often referred to as setting spaniels. The first person believed to have trained a spaniel-like dog to be a setter is the duke of Northumberland in the sixteenth century. Early setters were used with hunters who employed nets or falcons, but their purpose later evolved with the arrival of sporting guns.

The typical setter is a long-legged, lanky spaniel that is both cautious and self-disciplined. Today, setters are not seen serving as hunting dogs nearly as often, but their long-legged, graceful appearance makes them popular show dogs. The most commonly seen setters include the English setter and the Irish setter.

Ask and They Shall Retrieve

Almost all gun dogs are capable of bringing back shot game, but as different breeds began to have more clearly defined roles, a need arose for a special category of sporting dog just for retrieving game. Retrievers can bring back downed game from both land and water, but many breeds have become specialized as water dogs that primarily retrieve waterfowl that have fallen in lakes.

Retrievers are easy to train, are good-natured, and love to play, so they are very familiar to most people both as pets and common service animals. They usually have a "soft mouth," meaning they can carry quarry back to the hunter without damaging it. The quality of a soft mouth is one that must be trained, but it is much easier to train a dog that is genetically inclined to already have a soft mouth, as is the case with most retrievers. Because they have been bred to retrieve ducks from lakes and rivers, retrievers who are kept as pets love the water and love to play fetch. The most familiar of all are the Labrador retriever, or Lab, and the golden retriever.

The modern Labrador retriever was originally bred on the island of Newfoundland in eastern Canada. It descended from another species of dog called the St. John's water dog, which was bred on the island in the sixteenth century. Labs were originally used on Newfoundland to retrieve fishing nets. They have webbed feet to make them excellent swimmers. This comes in handy for retrieving game, such as duck and other waterfowl, from lakes. These dogs are highly intelligent and easy to train.

Another popular and very familiar retriever is the golden retriever, sometimes affectionately known as a goldie. These good-natured dogs are sensible, affectionate, and obedient companions. Like Labs, these dogs were bred to swim and fetch downed game. For this purpose they have a thick, water-repellent coat that provides warmth and an instinctive love of the water. The golden retriever was intentionally bred by a man named Sir Dudley Marjoribanks on his estate in Scotland in 1865. By selecting golden-coated puppies from the litters of several select breeds of retrievers, he eventually arrived at the stock for the modern golden retriever, which was officially recognized as a breed by the American Kennel Club in 1903.

Other familiar retrievers include the Chesapeake Bay retriever, and, somewhat surprisingly, the standard poodle. This showy, long-legged poodle was originally bred in Germany as a hunting dog. Its thick coat is water-resistant, which makes it an excellent swimmer. Poodles are still sometimes used in hunting today, although the American Kennel Club officially recognizes them in the category of "non-sporting dogs."

CHAPTER 5

Training and Caring for Hunting Dogs

Now that you have a good sense of what the different types of hunting dogs do and how they hunt, you may be wanting to find a hunting dog that is a good match for the type of hunting you would like to do. Remember that just because certain breeds of dogs have been bred to possess certain characteristics that lend themselves to hunting, these dogs are not automatically born hunters. They still must be trained to tap into their inbred instincts and make themselves useful to the hunter.

Choosing a Hunting Companion

Choosing a puppy to start training as your hunting partner is a big decision. The dog will be a part of your life for over a decade. Taking on ownership of any dog is a big responsibility and requires a lot of research and forethought. This is especially true of a hunting dog. You will want to choose a dog that will fit both your home life and suit the type of hunting you intend to do.

The first decision you must make is what breed to look at. You will want to independently research your chosen breed in greater depth to make sure you understand all of the pros and cons. Your research should help you understand what sort of health problems sometimes affect the breed, as well as other considerations like how much non-hunting exercise it will require. Reading books and reputable Web sites, such as the American Kennel Club's site, can help you learn more. It is also a good idea to talk to breeders that specialize in the breed in which you are interested.

A good breeder will keep his or her dogs in clean, well-maintained kennels. Use good judgment when examining both the dogs and their environment before choosing a breeder.

Choosing a good breeder is just as important as choosing a breed that is a perfect fit for your home and lifestyle. The first thing to do is ask veterinarians, groomers, boarding kennels, and other pet owners which breeders they know to be reputable. It's important to

A Day in the Life of a Hunter

Let's consider an average day on the hunt for a good hunter and his or her dog (or dogs). A hunter, depending on the game of choice, usually has to get up very early because that is when many game animals are most active. The hunter will make sure his or her dogs are fed and have had some water before leaving for the hunt. The dog should be eager and excited about the hunt—it is what it was bred to do—so if the dog seems uninterested, there could be something wrong. As part of gathering gear for the hunt, the hunter will make sure to have a first-aid kit and plenty of water for the dogs.

On the hunt, a lot of the job for both the hunter and the dog involves waiting and being quiet. A scenthound may search for a trail, but retrievers must sit and wait patiently and silently until receiving a command from the hunter. When game is plentiful and the hunt is successful, though, it can be a very exciting time and involve a lot of running around for the dog. A good hunter will check in with his or her dog to make sure it is not getting over-heated or dehydrated. Whether the hunt is successful or not, a good relationship between a hunter and his or her dog is an important bond. Any day spent out in the field or wilderness with a loyal companion and friend is a day well spent.

do your homework on this phase of the process, too. Many breeders are very knowledgeable about their breed and look out for the best interest of their dogs. However, some will pass themselves off as breeders when in reality they run puppy mills. A puppy mill is a large-scale commercial dog breeding operation where profit is prioritized over the well-being of the dogs.

To make sure the breeder is a good one, you will want to visit the breeder's home or kennel. The kennel should be clean and not smell bad. Avoid breeders who have large numbers of dogs and puppies kept in small spaces. This could be a puppy mill masquerading as a breeder. When you visit, ask to see the whole litter and at least one of the parents. The animals should look healthy and well fed and should not have runny eyes or noses. The puppies should be sociable and shouldn't display any fear toward the breeder. Ask a lot of questions of the breeder and pay attention to the questions he or she asks you. The breeder should be very knowledgeable about the breed. He or she should also ask questions about your home life and situation to make sure the dog will be given a good home. A good breeder will also want to keep a dog until it is at least six weeks old—and usually more like eight to twelve weeks. He or she will also be willing to provide references.

When it comes to actually choosing a puppy to train as your new hunting dog, look for a puppy that is not skittish or shy. An important characteristic for a hunting dog is that it not be frightened by loud noises. You can test its response to noises by getting low to the ground and making a loud sound. If the puppy runs away from you and doesn't return, it is probably not a good contender for a hunting dog. You can also ask the breeder to recommend a puppy to you based on your specific needs and situation. The breeder will have spent much more time with the puppies and should have a good sense of their individual personalities.

Training Your New Hunter

Training a dog to be a useful hunting companion must start with basic obedience training. You can then work up to more advanced skills that will be useful on the hunt. The first commands that every dog must learn are come, sit, and stay. Although these are very basic dog commands, they serve as the foundation for the more complex hunting commands to come later. Use food as a way to teach sitting. Hold food over the dog's head. Give the command to sit while pressing gently on the dog's hind legs. As soon as the dog sits, reward it with a treat. Repeat this over and over until your dog learns to sit as soon as you command it. The same system of positive reinforcement will work with most other commands. You will want to work with your dog every day, if possible, to make sure the lessons stay fresh.

As you begin more specific hunting dog training, you will want to slowly expose your dog to elements it will encounter on the hunt. If you are training a dog as a retriever, you

Here a hunter is seen working with a German shorthair to teach the dog how to flush a pigeon. Training sessions are important because even dogs that are bred to have certain hunting abilities must be taught the skills.

will want to start getting it used to water slowly. If you are training a flushing dog, you will want to make sure it can recognize the scent of waterfowl or the game it will be hunting. Continue to reward your dog when it does something correctly. There is nothing a dog wants more than to please its owner. To create a firm partnership with your dog, you want to establish early that good work will be rewarded.

You will want to work up to hunting with your dog very slowly. Expose your dog to actual hunting situations before taking it out into the field. A dog that is expected to perform around guns needs to be trained in the presence of guns so that it will not be surprised and unable to perform in action. Condition your dog prior to the hunt so that it will be able to perform at its best when you do take it out on its first hunt.

Keeping Your Dog Healthy

Part of maintaining a success-ful hunting partnership with your dog is making sure it is happy

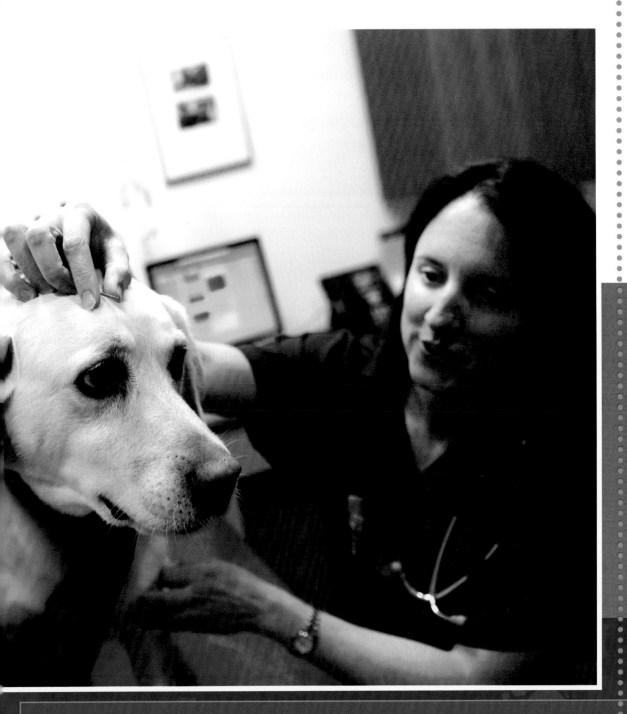

One of the most important parts of dog ownership, whether it is a pet or hunting companion, is taking your dog to a veterinarian for regular checkups.

and healthy. You will want to find a veterinarian to whom you can take your dog for annual checkups, even if nothing seems wrong. In between checkups, you can monitor your dog's health yourself. No one is more aware of your dog's health and behavior than you are. Make sure to be aware if anything changes in your dog's behavior that could be a sign of something wrong. Is it eating and drinking normally? Has its activity level changed? Does it have trouble going to the bathroom? The best way you can keep your dog healthy is to be on the lookout for any red flags.

Your dog can get sick just like you can, and hunting dogs are particularly prone to certain dangers. While out in the woods, your dog may be exposed to pests like fleas and ticks. In addition to being irritating to your dog, some of these parasites can carry diseases. Your veterinarian can provide you with medicines to give your dog monthly to help protect it from fleas and ticks. You should also make sure to keep your dog up to date on all vaccinations. A dog on the hunt is susceptible to a number of diseases. It is important to keep your dog's immune system strong and protected.

Another potential hazard for hunting dogs is snakebites. Depending on where you live and hunt, there may be poisonous snakes that can cause harm to your dog. Examine your dog for any unusual bite marks or cuts and scrapes it might have gotten while on the hunt. Catching small cuts early will keep them from getting infected. Always take a first-aid kit with you on the hunt so that you will be prepared if anything happens.

It is also important that your dog receives a balanced diet high in protein. Your dog will need high-quality food to give it energy and a healthy skeletal, muscular, and immune systems. You can ask your veterinarian for a recommendation on a good-quality food. Your dog should also have access to fresh drinking water at all times. Hunting dogs need more water than household dogs as their bodies exert more energy. When you are on the hunt, you should always bring water to give your dog to keep it from becoming dehydrated. Also, take care to keep the dog from overheating or getting too cold while on the hunt and at home. You must also make sure your dog has a safe, warm place to sleep. If you keep your dog in a kennel, make sure it is kept very clean, dry, well ventilated, and warm enough in the winter months. A hunting dog is a great help to a hunter, and it is important to train your dog well and keep it well maintained so that you can have the most successful hunts and rewarding experiences with your loyal companion and best friend.

GLOSSARY

agriculture The production of crops or livestock for food.

ammunition Bullets for guns.

breed To cause an animal to produce offspring in a controlled way.

burrow A hole in the ground made by an animal for shelter and habitation.

companion One that accompanies another; one that keeps company with another.

constellation A group of stars that form a pattern.

coursing Hunting with dogs to drive game forward.

dispatch To kill.

domesticate To tame a wild animal and train it to participate in and assist with human activities.

drag hunt When the scent of prey is dragged along a route, but no prey is actually hunted.

flush To scare game out of hiding.

game Animals being hunted.

grande vénerie Hunting for large game like deer with a pack of dogs.

groomer Someone who maintains the appearance of a dog's coat.

jackal A slender, long-legged wild dog.

nocturnal Mostly active at night.

parasite An organism that lives off of another and derives benefit at its host's expense.

petite vénerie Hunting for small game like rabbits or foxes with a pack of dogs.

prehistoric The time before written records of human activity.

prey An animal hunted or killed by another for food.

puppy mill A large-scale, commercial dog breeding operation where profit is prioritized over the well-being of the dogs.

quarry An animal pursued by a hunter or hunting dog.

retrieve To locate and bring in (especially killed or wounded game).

treeing To keep an animal up a tree until a hunter arrives.

vaccination Medicine taken as protection against a disease.

vermin A small, common, harmful or objectionable animal that is difficult to control, such as mice and rats.

American Dog Breeders Association (ADBA)

P.O. Box 1771

Salt Lake City, UT 84110

(801) 936-7513

Web site: http://www.adba.cc

The American Dog Breeders Association is committed to the preservation of the rights of dog owners and breeders. The ADBA was originally created for the registration of the American pit bull terrier but has since expanded to include information and registration for many other purebred dogs.

American Kennel Club (AKC)

260 Madison Avenue

New York, NY 10016

(212) 696-8200

Web site: http://www.akc.org

The American Kennel Club was founded in 1884 and is the official registry of purebred dog pedigree in the United States. It also promotes breed competitions like the annual Westminster Kennel Club Dog Show. Its Web site is a good source of information on different breeds.

Canadian Kennel Club (CKC)

200 Ronson Drive, Suite 400

Etobicoke, ON M9W 5Z9

Canada

(416) 675-5511

Web site: http://www.ckc.ca

Founded in 1888, the Canadian Kennel Club is the primary registry for pure-bred dog pedigrees in Canada. Beyond maintaining the pedigree registry, the CKC also promotes events such as dog shows and obedience trials for purebred dogs. Its Web site is a good source of information for all dog breed registers in Canada.

North American Gun Dog Association
7850 County Road 54
Burlington, CO 80807
(719) 342-0776
Web site: http://www.nagdog.com
The North American Gun Dog Association was formed to allow owners of bird dogs to hunt upland birds in a competitive format. It hosts a number of competitive events for hunting dogs each year beginning in September and culminating in a championship each April.

North American Hunting Retriever Association
P.O. Box 5159
Fredericksburg, VA 22403
(540) 899-7620
Web site: http://www.nahra.org
The North American Hunting Retriever Association was founded in 1983 to preserve the skills of a hunting retriever. It originated a set of standards and field tests to test retriever skills using realistic hunting scenarios. It has a number of local clubs and chapters in the United States and Canada.

North American Versatile Hunting Dog Association
P.O. Box 520
Arlington Heights, IL 60006
(847) 253-6488
Web site: http://www.navhda.org

The North American Versatile Hunting Dog Association is a nonprofit organization whose purpose is to foster, promote, and improve the versatile hunting dog breeds in North America. It seeks to conserve game by using well-trained, reliable hunting dogs. It also aids in the prevention of cruelty to animals by discouraging nonselective and uncontrolled breeding, which produces unwanted and uncared-for dogs.

Web Sites

Due to the changing nature of Internet links, Rosen Publishing has developed an online list of Web sites related to the subject of this book. This site is updated regularly. Please use this link to access this list:

http://www.rosenlinks.com/HUNT/Dogs

Bailey, Joan. *How to Help Gun Dogs Train Themselves: Taking Advantage of Early Conditioned Training.* Portland, OR: Swan Valley Press, 2008.

De Vito, Dominique. *The Encyclopedia of Dog Breeds: A Field Guide to 231 Dog Breeds and Varieties.* Neptune, NJ: TFH Publications, 2011.

Dokken, Tom. *Retriever Training: The Complete Guide to Developing Your Hunting Dog.* Iola, WI: Krause Publications, 2009.

Frain, Sean. *Working Terriers.* London, England: Quiller Press, 2008.

Hancock, David. *Sporting Terriers: Their Form, Their Function, and Their Future.* London, England: Crowood Press, 2012.

Hartley, Oliver. *Hunting Dogs.* Columbus, OH: A. R. Harding Press, 2010.

Johnson, Chuck. *Training the Versatile Hunting Dog.* Belgrade, MT: Wilderness Adventure Press, 2009.

Klein, Adam. *Hunting* (Outdoor Adventure). Edina, MN: Checkerboard Books, 2008.

Mattinson, Pippa. *Total Recall: Perfect Response Training for Puppies and Adult Dogs.* London, England: Quiller Press, 2012.

McRae, Sloane. *Upland Hunting: Pheasant, Quail, and Other Game.* New York, NY: Rosen Publishing, 2010.

McRae, Sloane. *Waterfowl Hunting.* New York, NY: Rosen Publishing, 2010.

Morrison, Paul. *Hunting with Spaniels: Training Your Flushing Dog.* New York, NY: Kennel Club Books, 2012.

Petersen, Judy Monroe. *Varmint Hunting.* New York, NY: Rosen Publishing, 2011.

Roebuck, Kenneth. *Gun Dog Training: Spaniels and Retrievers.* Mechanicsburg, PA: Stackpole Books, 2011.

Roettgur, Anthony Z. *Urban Gun Dogs: Training Flushing Dogs for Home and Field.* New York, NY: Benjamin Schleider, 2011.

Shellhass, Dave, and Stephen Shellhass. *Outdoor Kids Club Ultimate Hunting Guide.* Greenville, OH: Miami Valley Outdoor Media, 2011.

BIBLIOGRAPHY

American Kennel Club. "Registered Breeds." Retrieved January 2012 (http://www.akc.org).

Coile, Caroline. *The Dog Breed Bible.* Hauppauge, NY: Barron's Educational Services, 2007.

Coppinger, Raymond, and Lorna Coppinger. *Dogs: A Startling New Understanding of Canine Origin, Behavior, and Evolution.* New York, NY: Scribner, 2001.

Dahl, Amy. "The Genetics of Colors in Labradors." GunDogsOnline.com, April 2010. Retrieved January 2012 (http://www.gundogsonline.com/Article/the-genetics-of-color-in-labradors-Page1.htm).

Elman, Robert. *Hunting Allies.* Broomall, PA: Mason Crest, 2002.

Fergus, Charles. *Gun Dog Breeds: A Guide to Spaniels, Retrievers, and Pointing Dogs.* Guilford, CT: The Lyons Press, 2002.

King, H. H. *Working Terriers, Badgers, and Badger Digging.* London, England: Read Books, 2005.

Krassler, David. "Hunting Family Companion or Kennel Dog." GunDogsOnline.com, June 2011. Retrieved January 2012 (http://www.gundogsonline.com/Article/hunting-dog-family-companion-or-kennel-dog-Page1.htm).

Lamb, Vicki. *The Ultimate Hunting Dog Reference Book.* Guilford, CT: The Lyons Press, 2006.

Morris, Desmond. *Dogs: A Dictionary of Dog Breeds.* North Pomfret, VT: Trafalgar Square Publishing, 2002.

Palika, Liz. *The Howell Book of Dogs: The Definitive Reference to 300 Breeds and Varieties.* New York, NY: Howell Book House, 2007.

Recum, Andres Von. *Hunting with Hounds in North America.* New York, NY: Pelican Publishing, 2002.

Smith, Steve. *The Encyclopedia of North American Sporting Dogs.* Minocqua, MI: Willow Creek Press, 2002.

Wang, Xiaoming, and Richard H. Tedford. *Dogs: Their Fossil Relatives and Evolutionary History.* New York, NY: Columbia University Press, 2008.

Weaver, Richard. *Training Your Pointing Dog for Hunting & Home.* Mechanicsburg, PA: Stackpole Books, 2007.

Wimpole, Justin. *First Aid for Dogs.* London, England: New Holland Publishers, 2005.

INDEX

About the Author

Susan Meyer is an author living and working in New York City. Meyer has an avid interest in dogs, both in terms of professional research and wished-for ownership. Sadly, city living does not currently allow her to have a dog, but she does own a cat named Dinah, who is as close to a terrier in personality as felinely possible.

About the Consultant

Benjamin Cowan has more than twenty years of both big game and small game hunting experience. In addition to being an avid hunter, Cowan is also a member of many conservation organizations. He currently resides in west Tennessee.

Photo Credits

Cover, pp. 1, 3 © Andre Babiak Photography/Alamy; pp. 5, 16 Chris Furlong/ Getty Images; p. 7 Alfredo Dagli Orti/The Art Archive at Art Resource, NY; p. 8 iStockphoto/Thinkstock; pp.10–11 Massimo Pizzotti/Photographer's Choice/Getty Images; pp. 20–21 Press Association via Associated Press; pp. 22–23, 32, 38–39, 48–49 © AP Images; p. 27 © Adrian Sherratt/Alamy; pp. 28–29 Edwin Megargee/ National Geographic Image Collection/Getty Images; p. 35 © Jeffrey S. Adams/ Alamy; pp. 40–41 Sun Sentinel/MCT/Getty Images; p. 45 The Washington Post/ Getty Images; pp. 50–51 New York Daily News Archive/Getty Images; cover and interior (camouflage patterns) © iStockphoto.com/molotovcoketail; back cover and interior background (landscape) iStockphoto/Thinkstock; back cover and interior (figure silhouettes) Hemera/Thinkstock; back cover (grass silhouette) iStockphoto.com/Makhnach_M; interior (figure silhouette) © iStockphoto.com/ Michael Olson.

Designer: Nicole Russo; Photo Researcher: Amy Feinberg